Invasion of the Comet People

○○○○○○○○○○○○○○○○○○○○○○○○○○○○○○

by PHILIP CURTIS

Text illustrations by Tony Ross

Alfred A. Knopf ○ *New York*

This is a Borzoi Book published by Alfred A. Knopf, Inc.

First U.S. Edition, 1983
Text copyright © 1981 by Philip Curtis
Illustrations copyright © 1981 by
Andersen Press Limited
Cover illustration copyright © 1983 by
Margaret Gilbert

Originally published in Great Britain as *Mr. Bowser and
the Comet Crisis* by Andersen Press Limited, London.

Manufactured in the United States of America
10 9 8 7 6 5 4 3 2 1

Library of Congress Cataloging in Publication Data
Curtis, Philip.
Invasion of the comet people. (Capers)
Previously published as: Mr. Browser and
the comet crisis. 1981.
Summary: Spiky discovers that his new friend Jason
and his parents are an outer-space family from
Halley's comet and that their plans pose grave danger
to the Earth. [1. Extraterrestrial beings—Fiction.
2. Science fiction. 3. Halley's comet—Fiction]
I. Ross, Tony, ill. II. Title. III. Series.
PZ7.C9483Io 1983 [Fic] 82-9923
ISBN 0-394-85490-X   ISBN 0-394-95490-4 (lib. bdg.)

Contents

○○○○○○○○○○○○○○○○○○○○○○○○○○○○○○○○○○○

INVASION OF THE COMET PEOPLE

A Strange Arrival

○○○○○○○○○○○○○○○○○○○○○○○○○○○○○○○○ ○○

A boy, a man, and a woman came in from the sea across the mudbanks at the mouth of a long, large river. The bare feet of the walkers sent ripples across dark pools of water and brought mud to the surface. The walkers could not see the ripples or the mud because it was still before dawn.

All three had their shoes slung around their necks. The man had his trousers turned up to his knees. The boy said something to his father, and the man stopped abruptly.

"English!" he said fiercely. "Only English from now on!" He spoke without any accent, like a TV announcer. The boy nodded his head obediently.

Each one of them was carrying a suitcase. Inside the boy's case were a couple of books to write in, a few clothes, and a bag of mar-

bles. His mother's case held mostly clothes. His father's, which was by far the biggest, contained a large box and many packets of ten-dollar bills—a total of $50,000.

The man was anxious to reach the river-bank beach, the woman was worried about her feet, and the boy was enjoying the walk. He liked the squishing and oozing of the mud between his toes and the funny feeling of his feet sinking. As they neared the edge the mud became thicker. They couldn't pick up their feet without making sucking sounds.

"Stop playing around!" complained the man when the boy bent over and picked up a frog. He balanced the frog on his suitcase until it jumped off and plopped back into the water.

Lights were coming on as early workers were waking up and preparing for the day.

"That should be Burryville ahead of us," said the man, pointing to a cluster of lights.

"What's that?" asked the boy, pointing to a dark construction which stretched out over the mud away to their left.

"According to our probe, it should be the south dock," said the man. "It's marked as a landmark to guide us. We should move toward it a little. The army owns some of the land to our right. We don't want to come up there."

"Sometimes I wish," began the woman, eager to speak her first words of English, "I wish—"

She was interrupted by a strange, high pitched sound which came from deep in the boy's throat. He had stepped on the sharp edge of a rock.

His father growled, "The next time that happens, say 'ow.' Say it now!"

"Ow!" cried the boy, his face still wrinkled with pain.

"That's better," said his father. "Remember, you must make the right sounds even when unexpected things happen."

"You're hard on him," said the woman.

"I have to be hard on us all," declared her husband, "or we won't survive here very long."

They walked on silently. The boy was putting his feet down carefully now. The dawn began to break as they walked along a stretch of flat land by the river.

A fisherman, out early to dig for bait while the river was still low, came toward them.

"What a nuisance!" muttered the man. "Somebody's seen us! If only we could have reached this point in darkness! By my calculations, there should have been another hour to go.

"Leave all the talking to me," said the man as the fisherman began waving to them.

"Hello, there!" the fisherman shouted to them. "Did you see that strange light out there? Came down like a rocket. A few seconds later it shot up again into the sky and disappeared!"

"Can't say I saw anything," the man shouted back. "Perhaps we were still on our friend's boat."

The fisherman looked at them suspiciously in the gray light.

"Perhaps a boat fired a rocket," suggested the boy. His father frowned at him.

"A rocket?" repeated the fisherman. "On a river? I've never seen anything like that. Where d'you say you're from?"

"We've been out on a boat with friends," explained the man. "The boy, here, didn't feel very well, so they let us off. I want to get him home as soon as possible."

"He looks pale," agreed the fisherman. Then he asked doubtfully, "Where's the boat now?"

"On the other side of the dock," replied the man.

"Well, I won't keep you. I have to dig some bait before I go to work today."

The fisherman moved away with a puzzled look on his face. He looked back at the group once or twice as they headed for the beach.

"Hurry up!" muttered the man to his son. "He's accepted our story for the moment, but we must vanish as quickly as we can in case he changes his mind!"

New to
the Neighborhood 2

○○○○○○○○○○○○○○○○○○○○○○○○○ **2** ○○

"Where are we going?" asked the boy, who was now panting in his efforts to keep up with his parents.

"There are shelters along the riverbank. We'll have to sit in one of them and dry off our feet. Then we'll make our way along the river front and catch the first bus out of town."

The boy looked puzzled. The word "shelter" was only a verb in his vocabulary. But he soon found out what his father meant. As they picked their way up toward the road, climbing some stone steps, they spotted a small broken-down building.

Inside, his mother took a towel from her case, and they dried off their feet. The boy put on shoes and socks and stared out at the light now shining on the water.

"Neat," he said, and his father smiled.

"We should be pleased it's not raining," he remarked. "When you're ready, we'll start walking in the direction of the dock. According to my instructions, a bus will be coming along later on. Look, there's a sign over there that says 'Bus Stop.' "

"Let's stand there," said the boy, but his father shook his head.

"You've a great deal to learn," he said. "That sign is for buses going in the other direction. We must look for a sign on this side of the road."

"I forgot that their cars travel on the right," said the boy.

"Mary, do you have plenty of small change?" the man asked. "They tell me you have to pay the exact amount of money on these buses."

His wife laughed. "Seems funny to be called Mary," she said. "Yes, I've plenty of change."

"I shall buy three tickets to the end of the route, and we'll have a look around as we go."

"We must be looking for something," said the boy.

"Of course. We're looking for a quiet little town where we can bury ourselves for a while. And it must have a reasonably pleasant school, of course."

"School!" grumbled the boy. "This world looks so interesting. Do I have to go to school?"

"Afraid so," said his father. "If you didn't, that would look suspicious. We three have to fit in naturally. And school's a good place for you to make friends."

"I do like this gravity," said the woman as they made their way along the road. "I could walk and walk, and I'm sure my feet wouldn't hurt me one bit."

"It's a degree or two less than ours," said her husband. "But please don't refer to the past again. We must remember that we come from Endfield. You know all the details by heart. See that you don't slip up."

They walked steadily along the river front until they reached the beginning of the dock. There were a few people standing around. One was a boy who was just starting his newspaper rounds.

"Excuse me," said the man politely, "can you tell me where the bus station is?"

The boy directed them, and in twenty minutes they were making a choice of buses. The man chose one which had the name of a town on the front, instead of one which was heading for a street. They climbed aboard along with the early workers.

"End of the route, please," said the man to the driver, and his wife provided him with some of her change to make up the exact fare.

"You been to the mint lately?" asked the driver with a smile when he saw the bright new coins in front of him.

For a second the man hesitated, puzzled, then quipped back, "No, the bank. I'm a good customer."

"You must be," observed the driver, laughing. Soon the journey began. They drove through the town, with shops and houses lining the road for miles. At last there was a little countryside, with green fields and trees, and even a few fields of corn. Then more houses. The bus stopped in the middle of a little town.

"Shall we get out?" asked the boy. He was getting tired of the bus ride. But he could see that his father was pleased with what they were able to see.

"Not just yet," his father answered. "I want to see a little more."

Soon they were coming out on the other side of the town, past the church and the police station. Down a hill, ahead of them was a school. By now it was nearly eight o'clock, and already there were a few children in the playground. One or two of them were swinging on a jungle gym like well-trained monkeys.

"There's your school," said the man. "A large field and a swimming pool. Plenty of room to move around. What more can you want? Do you like the area, Mary?"

"Looks reasonable," replied his wife.

"Most of these people probably go to and from the city every day," said the man. "And they come home at night too tired to bother about anything except their television programs. This will make a nice little hideout for us."

He stood up and went across to the driver.

"Will you let us out at the next stop, please?"

"But you wanted the end of the route," argued the driver. "There are still two towns to go."

"Never mind. I've changed my mind. This will do fine," replied the man.

"Okay, buddy," said the driver.

The three of them left the bus and walked back in the direction of the school. When they reached it, they saw its name on the board by the gate.

CHIVVY CHASE ELEMENTARY SCHOOL

Mr. B. Sage, Principal

"I'll go and speak to the principal tomorrow. You can start school next week," said the man. "Now we must find a place to stay for a few days while we look for a house to rent."

The boy looked curiously at his future friends as they played on the jungle gym.

"I could do better than that," he said. "My feet feel so light and springy down here."

"Now don't start showing off as soon as you enter that playground," his father warned him. "And if I were you, I wouldn't start playing marbles, either. I know what you're like when you're in the mood. Safer not to play at all."

"Oh, Dad!" protested the boy. He looked so upset that his father laughed.

"Well, maybe one or two games," he said. "But for goodness sake, be sensible!"

Meanwhile Mr. Browser, the teacher of the children who were the boy's age, was hurrying to finish off his bacon and eggs. He didn't know that in just a few days an unusual new student would be added to his class.

The Marbles Marvel

○○○○○○○○○○○○○○○○○○○○○○○○○○○○○ ○○

3

Spiky Jackson arrived early at school Monday morning. His mother had to take the car into the repair shop before going to work, so she dropped him off.

Spiky's hair was lying flat, freshly plastered with water, and his shoes and shirt were neat and clean. He often looked like this at the beginning of the school day. Sometimes the neatness lasted for about half an hour. Then his hair began to stand up in a spiky way, his shirttail hung over his jeans, and he became the normal Spiky Jackson all his friends knew.

Spiky was first on the playground, and he decided to practice marbles. He rolled one marble across the playground and then tried to hit it with another one. All of the slopes and the holes in the playground made the game a difficult one. This must be much harder than playing golf, Spiky thought. He watched in dismay as his second marble trickled farther and farther away from the first one.

"That's not bad shooting," said a voice behind him. "But you should have allowed more for the slope."

Spiky straightened up quickly because he didn't recognize the voice. But when he saw who it was, he relaxed a little. A boy, smaller than himself and with spindly legs, stood looking at him. He had a mop of curly, light hair, freckles, and big front teeth.

His eyes were as blue as the bluest of Spiky's marbles. He stared at Spiky sharply, as if he knew that his piercing eyes were his best feature.

"Playing planets?" he asked.

"Planets?" said Spiky. "What's that? I'm just practicing with a couple of marbles."

"Yes, of course," said the boy hastily. "Some of us called the game 'planets' where I come from."

"Where do you come from?" demanded

Spiky. "You're new, aren't you?"

"Yes. We've come from a small town called Endfield."

"Endfield? Never heard of it. Where's that?" asked Spiky.

The boy was surprised and confused for a moment because Spiky didn't know something he had been expected to know. "Out West, you know," he said. "My father came and saw the principal last week."

"Did old Sage say which class you'd be in?"

"Yes. Mr. Browser's class." replied the boy.

"That's my class."

"Good. What's the school like?"

"All right." Spiky said. "Plenty of swimming and football and school trips, if you go for that sort of thing."

The new boy shrugged his shoulders. "How may pl—marbles do you have?"

"I brought ten to school today. I've got twenty more at home. I never bring them all. Some people try to swipe marbles if you're not careful. Do you have any?"

The boy stared at Spiky's marbles. They looked so inviting!

"I have a few," he said. "I've brought one along. My father doesn't like me playing marbles."

Spiky was going to ask why, but he was distracted by the marble. It was beautiful, shot through with colors.

"Wow! I've never seen one like that!" said Spiky. "What's your name?"

"Jason Taylor," the boy answered. "What's yours?"

"I'm Simon Jackson, usually called Spiky. Want to play a game?"

Jason was doubtful.

"Come on," said Spiky, ready to make a generous opening offer. "We'll play for a while, and I'll give you your marble back at the end if you lose it."

Spiky rolled one of his marbles and challenged Jason to hit it. At first Jason aimed to hit Spiky's in one shot. But he changed his mind and rolled his own just about a yard ahead of him.

"Tactics," said Spiky approvingly. He decided to risk an outright hit. But his marble rolled yards beyond Jason's.

"Bad luck," said Jason. Then Spiky saw those sharp blue eyes narrow in steely concentration.

Jason's marble seemed to spin as it left his hand. It swerved away, and Spiky began to look forward to his next throw. But then it swerved back again, right on course! Slowing down, it ended by resting against Spiky's marble with a gentle click.

"Man!" shouted Spiky. "What luck!"

"Yeah," Jason agreed. "Let's play again."

They played again, and again. Soon Spiky

had lost eight of his ten marbles.

"We'd better stop now," said Jason. "Other boys are coming."

Hastily he pushed the marbles he had won back into Spiky's pocket. Spiky wasn't at all sorry to stop playing.

Barry Sibbett walked over. He was about the biggest boy in the school. Barry had seen the marbles, and he challenged Spiky to a game. If Barry wanted to play, it could be dangerous to refuse. So Spiky played, but he lost steadily. Jason, along with a group of other kids, watched every move. Spiky was looking worse and worse. Suddenly Jason spoke up.

"I'll play you for the marbles Spiky's lost," he told Barry.

"Who are you?" asked Barry. "A new kid?"

"Yes," said Jason. "Who throws first?"

"I will." Barry smiled craftily, thinking that he hadn't even had to toss to go first. He rolled one of his oldest marbles and waited confidently.

Jason bent down. In a flash his marble

was spinning on its way. It looked like it was off course. Barry was rubbing his hands. Then it swerved and ended up hitting Barry's fair and square.

"One," said Jason, and handed Spiky the marble. Barry scowled and played again. He lost again. The other kids were enjoying this more than Barry could stand. Short or long distances made no difference to Jason. His shots were on target every time. Soon Spiky had all his lost marbles back in his pocket again.

"Let's play a different game," muttered Barry. But just then the bell rang, and everyone stood still. Barry glared at Jason, and Jason stared right back at him out of those blue eyes.

"Hey, thanks," whispered Spiky as they walked into school. "You saved me. Here, I'll give you a couple."

"No! No!" Jason said, shrinking back. "I shouldn't have played."

Spiky was surprised. He didn't know what to say.

As they walked into school Jason stared at his new surroundings. He was glad to be following Spiky into the classroom.

The principal was busily talking to Mr. Browser. As soon as Mr. Sage saw Jason he called him over. "This is Jason Taylor, Mr. Browser," he said. He spoke loudly, as principals always do when they want children to overhear what they are saying. "He comes with a good record from his old school in Endfield, according to his father, though we haven't received the details yet. He's going to work hard here, too, I hope."

"I'll try," said Jason. He shook hands with Mr. Browser who pointed out an empty desk at the back for him.

"I'll give you some books in a minute," he said.

Jason was disappointed because his new friend, Spiky, sat right in the front. He didn't know that Mr. Browser did that on purpose because Spiky sometimes found it hard to concentrate on his work. So it was Spiky who was able to hear what the principal, Mr. Sage, went on to tell Mr. Browser.

"Funny little guy," observed Mr. Sage. "You know, his father seemed mostly concerned about one thing. He tried to persuade me to forbid the boy to play marbles. He called him a 'marbles addict,' and said it could interfere with his work and get him into trouble."

"They're all marbles addicts at times," Mr. Browser said, laughing. "It's the big game these days. As long as they don't play during class, it doesn't bother me."

"They'd better not play in class!" declared Mr. Sage sharply.

"Well, did you forbid him?" asked Mr. Browser.

"Of course not. Some parents are so ridiculous! The father accepted my decision, but he didn't like it. Muttered something about hoping I wouldn't regret it! Can you believe it? What next! Well, they're all yours. Calm them down, will you?" Mr. Sage strode out with more important matters on his mind.

Trouble Shooting 4

4

Jason settled in fairly well at school. He lost some of the respect he had gained with his marbles game when he turned out to be hopeless at football. All he cared about was avoiding injury. But after a few days something happened at recess that turned Jason into a kind of hero. It also changed his mind about playing marbles.

A roly-poly first grader, who was spoiled and had plenty of toys, dropped a bag of marbles on the ground. They rolled in all directions. As he started to pick them up Barry Sibbett came along and started picking them up, too. This was a bad sign for the little first grader. Sure enough, the little boy started crying when he counted his marbles. He was ten marbles short.

"Barry's kept them," other kids told him.

But that didn't help because no one was brave enough to try to get them back for him.

"Lend me two marbles," said Jason suddenly. "Maybe I can win them back for you." Doubtfully the first grader handed over two marbles.

Jason hunted Barry down. "Challenge you to a game!" he said.

Barry couldn't believe his luck would run against him again, so he accepted. Within a few minutes he had lost most of the marbles he had stolen from the first grader. Jason's throwing was deadly accurate. He never missed.

The other kids watched in silence as Barry slunk away and Jason gave all the marbles he had won back to the little boy.

"Jason," said Spiky, "you're great at marbles. Why don't you play more often? You'd win hundreds of them!"

Jason just gave him a curious look. He might have resisted other temptations to play, but the little first grader changed all that by coming to school the next morning with a small bag full of brand new marbles.

"These are for you," he said to Jason. "My mom said you should have them because you stood up to a bully for me."

Jason took them, stared into the bag, and jangled the marbles around with his fingers. Spiky was watching, and he saw Jason's steely blue eyes gleam.

"Thanks very much," said Jason. "I think I'll start playing after all."

In fact, Jason played in every spare minute. He won marbles that day from everyone who challenged him. By the end of the day both his pockets were bulging. Spiky Jackson ran after him on the way home from school.

"How many have you won, Jason?" he asked.

"Seventy-six," answered Jason calmly.

"What's your dad going to say?"

"I won't tell him," said Jason. "I'll hide them in the shed in my backyard."

"What if he finds them?"

"Oh, he'll be angry, take them all away, I guess. But I'll make sure he doesn't. Are you going to bring some more marbles tomorrow?"

"Oh, I guess so," said Spiky, surprised.

"I'll play you for them," Jason said.

Suddenly two boys dashed past them. Spiky recognized Barry Sibbett and his friend, Gary Deakins. When they were a few yards ahead they stopped short and turned around.

"Look out! We've got trouble!" said Spiky. Jason looked around him as if he didn't know where the trouble could be coming from.

Barry walked back and stood right in Jason's way. Gary stayed a few feet behind Barry.

"Let's have those marbles back, Jason. You know you cheated, anyway," said Barry.

"I didn't cheat!" cried Jason, still unaware of the danger facing him. "I can't help it if I'm a better player than you are."

Gary Deakins laughed. This new boy had

just said the one thing that would annoy Barry the most. He was asking for trouble! Spiky Jackson realized this, too. He clenched his fists anxiously.

"Hand them over!" Barry demanded.

"Why should I?" asked Jason innocently.

Barry thrust his face close to Jason's. "Just hand them over!"

"No!" cried Jason.

Spiky knew what was coming. Barry smashed his fist into Jason's cheek. "Hand them over!" he repeated.

Jason shook his head, feeling his cheek sting.

"Then here goes!" cried Barry. His friend, Gary, who thought Jason was easy prey, joined in the attack. They forced Jason to the ground. Soon the bigger boys would have the marbles. But when Spiky saw that Barry was off guard for a second, he knocked Barry sideways into Gary. Then Spiky delivered a couple of good blows before Barry and Gary could pull themselves together again.

Just then a big man came along. "Cut it

out, you boys," he warned them. "Or I'll have to drag you apart myself."

Barry and Gary picked themselves up and ran back toward the school. But first they gave Spiky and Jason looks that spelled more trouble.

"Spiky," said Jason, his blue eyes for once looking almost kind, "you're a good friend."

"I did what I could," said Spiky. "They're bullies."

"I didn't expect to find a friend like you in this world," added Jason. Then he turned away sharply, as if he regretted something he had said.

"It's not such a bad world," said Spiky, laughing. When Jason turned to face him again, Spiky could see that Jason's cheek was already showing the bruise—green and yellow and purple.

"You got a nice one there," he commented. "My bruises usually take days to come out in colors."

"I have sensitive skin," mumbled Jason. He covered his cheek with his hand. Spiky thought again of his words "in this world." Very odd words, thought Spiky, and being Spiky, he blurted out his suspicions.

"Jason," he asked curiously, "do you really come from Endfield? You never talk about your old school or your home."

Jason's eyes narrowed. "No. I don't come from Endfield, Spiky. And I can't tell you any more, even if you are my friend! Please don't ask me to. See you tomorrow!"

Jason turned and ran off. He was yards away before Spiky had finished thinking about what he had said.

More Marbles

○○○○○○○○○○○○○○○○○○○○○○○○○○○○○ ○○

5

Each day Spiky Jackson waited for Jason to reveal where he had come from. But once or twice when Spiky tried to question him, Jason turned away. It seemed like Jason could guess Spiky's question before he even asked it.

After a while Spiky lost interest in the mystery. He had something more absorbing to think about now—Jason was playing marbles all the time.

Every day at recess, those icy blue eyes concentrated, and the marbles swerved and stopped and hit their targets. It was as if Jason had some sort of radar control over them.

At the end of the day Jason's pockets were always bulging with marbles he had won. Some kids stopped bringing marbles to school and played other games. The older and bigger kids didn't like losing to this skinny newcomer. Jason just sucked in their marbles like a vacuum cleaner eats up crumbs.

"Jason," Spiky begged him, "why don't you stop playing for a while? Some bully is going to pick a terrible fight with you soon."

"Why should I stop?" Jason replied. "I play fairly. I don't force them to play. It's not my fault if they lose."

That's a strange thing to say, thought Spiky. Of course it's Jason's fault that they lose! His marbles will do anything for him. They even curve around corners if he wants them to.

There was a feverish look in Jason's eyes these days. And as Spiky expected, trouble came Jason's way before long.

"Jason," said Barry Sibbett at recess one morning, "the rest of the class has chosen me to challenge you to a game of marbles. We've collected fifty marbles. The loser of the game hands over his fifty at the end."

"I don't have fifty here," said Jason.

"So bring them in tomorrow if you lose. Okay?"

Six other big kids were supporting Barry, so Jason really couldn't refuse if he wanted to. A crowd gathered round. Kids gave up their football and hopscotch to come and watch the duel.

"It's like a shoot-out in a Western," said Anna Cardwell. "The stakes are high."

There would be ten short games, and the player with the most hits out of ten would be declared the official winner and get the fifty marbles.

Jason was nervous at the start—or pretended to be—and his shots were bad. Barry won the first hit, and his friends clapped and cheered. Jason got annoyed, and Spiky recognized the usual signs as Jason frowned and pursed his lips. It looked like he was calling on extra powers of concentration.

Then the marbles started to obey him. Barry lost by nine hits to one, and the fifty marbles passed into Jason's bulging pockets.

Everyone waited to see what Barry and his friends would do. Only Anna dared to speak.

"You'd better collect fifty more and try again!" she mocked Barry. Then she darted away as Barry scowled at her.

"Better watch out!" Spiky warned Jason. "There could be trouble. Barry doesn't like losing one marble, let alone fifty!"

At that point the bell rang for the end of recess. As they walked into school Spiky had more advice for his mysterious friend.

"If I were you, I'd hand over those marbles to Mr. Browser for safe keeping until after school," he said. "Otherwise Barry and his friends might steal them back."

At first Jason seemed to ignore Spiky's advice. But perhaps Spiky's earnest expression and the earlier threats from Barry and Gary helped to change his mind.

"All right, Spiky. I'll let Mr. Browser hold them," he agreed.

When they got back to class, Mr. Browser was just finishing his chart of the Battle of Hastings on the blackboard. They were doing a unit on famous battles in other countries.

Mr. Browser had read about and taught the Battle of Hastings so many times that Spiky and his friends thought that Mr. Browser probably could have won the war himself. He always pointed out the mistakes King Harold made that cost the Saxons their victory.

The Battle of Hastings was Mr. Browser's favorite battle in history. He wanted the whole class to be as excited about it as he was. His chart was split up into four phases of the battle, and he intended to explain them to the class as soon as they had settled down.

Jason stood by Mr. Browser's desk while Mr. Browser was putting the final touches to King Harold's defenses at the top of the hill. Jason rattled the marbles in his pocket, and Mr. Browser turned, chalk in hand, looking irritable.

"What is it, Jason?" he asked.

"Please, Mr. Browser, would you look after my marbles for me until after school?"

"All right. Put them on my desk."

Mr. Browser turned to the blackboard again. Jason coughed. "Hurry up, Jason."

"There are too many to put on top of the desk, Mr. Browser. There's no room for them all."

Mr. Browser put down his chalk and looked at Jason. "Hand them over," he said. "I'll put them inside the desk, then."

Mr. Browser always preferred to have marbles in his desk rather than rolling around in the desks of his students. Jason began to bail out his winnings. The class watched, fascinated, as Mr. Browser had to put handful after handful into the desk.

"Been winning a lot, eh, Jason?" he said as he closed the drawer on the last marble.

"Yes, Mr. Browser."

As Jason went to his place something was troubling Mr. Browser. He remembered what Mr. Sage had said about Jason's father not liking him to play marbles. Very curious, thought Mr. Browser with one more glance at the strange new boy.

History Holds
a Clue

ooooooooooooooooooooooooooooo **6** oo

"Now take out your history books, all of you," said Mr. Browser. "Find the chapter on the Norman Conquest. We'll refer to that as we go along. I promised you I'd explain all about the Battle of Hastings today. So first look at the board. . . ."

Mr. Browser was away on a subject he knew inside out. Even Anna found the description of the battle mildly interesting, especially when Mr. Browser described the part played by the poor horses. But Jason wasn't interested at all. Even the deaths on the battlefield, dramatically described by Mr. Browser, bored him. His mind was still on all the marbles he had won.

Then Mr. Browser told them to open their textbooks to a page with a picture of funny little people sailing in ships and fighting

with bows and arrows. Mr. Browser began explaining the picture in detail.

Anna's hand shot up. "Mr. Browser, what's that sort of hairy monster up in the sky? Some of the people in the picture are looking at it."

"Ah, yes," said Mr. Browser. "Who knows what Anna's hairy monster really is?"

Selwyn Jordan raised his hand. "It's a comet, Mr. Browser."

"Exactly, Selwyn. Shortly before the battle, the Saxons saw this bright comet in the sky, and they were very worried about it. When the battle was lost and King Harold was killed, some people said that the comet had been a warning of bad times to come."

Mr. Browser's wandering eyes chanced upon Jason. From being completely bored, Jason was now so absorbed that he seemed to be shivering as he stared at the picture of the comet.

"Perhaps we should spend a little time talking about comets another day," said Mr. Browser. But Selwyn was bursting with information.

"That same comet is supposed to be coming near the earth again in 1986," he declared. "It's called Halley's Comet."

"Supposed to be?" called out Jason. "I know it's coming. It's on its way—" He stopped as suddenly as he had spoken. He covered his face with his hands, as if he wished he hadn't opened his mouth.

"That's right," said Mr. Browser in surprise. "No doubt it's on its way. It last appeared in 1910, and it appears about every seventy-five years. How did you happen to know that, Jason?"

Mr. Browser was not surprised that Selwyn had known, because Selwlyn was usually a gold mine of information on science. But Jason's outburst was quite a surprise. Now suddenly Jason seemed determined not to say any more. He kept his face hidden and just shook his head from side to side.

"Are you all right, Jason?" he asked. Jason was staring straight ahead now, making no effort to copy Mr. Browser's Battle of Hastings chart.

"Yes, thank you," replied Jason, and with a jerk he tried to put his mind to his work.

Mr. Browser decided that this was one of those occasions when it would be wiser not to ask any further questions. Jason's behavior was odd, but Mr. Browser was so used to children behaving oddly that he knew it was often best to just "wait and see." However, when he met Mr. Sage in the hall at the end of the morning, he still had Jason on his mind.

"That Jason Taylor is an unusual boy," he observed.

"Hmmm," said the principal who, as usual, had something else on his mind.

"Yes, he's been playing marbles and he's won an awful lot."

"Marbles?" asked Mr. Sage.

"Yes, you remember his father's strange attitude? Also, when I was talking about comets he really began to act strange."

"Marbles? Comets?" repeated the principal in disbelief. "I'm afraid I have more important things to consider at the moment. Tomorrow we are being visited by the superintendent. I've told him what an active school we have here, so I hope you'll make sure that your class shows signs of activity."

"They're usually pretty active," said Mr. Browser jokingly.

The principal didn't even smile. "You know what I mean," he said, and walked away.

Jason's unusual behavior had made most of the class very curious about him. Spiky had only been able to look back at him a few times, but he couldn't help noticing how the blood had drained from Jason's face when the word "comet" was mentioned. At lunch he walked out to the playground with Jason and Selwyn.

"What's upset you, Jason?" Spiky asked bluntly. "Don't you like comets?"

Before Jason could answer, Selwyn was treating them to some of his scientific knowledge.

"You can't be afraid of comets, Jason," he explained. "They're as near to being nothing as anything can be, if you know what I mean. Some comets can pass right across the earth without disturbing anything. There are some gases in the tails of comets, but that's about all."

"I'm not afraid of comets," said Jason, sounding angry.

"Then what's the matter, Jason?" Spiky persisted.

"I don't want to talk about it at all," said Jason. "Let's go and play football."

That's even stranger! thought Spiky. Jason usually avoided playing football whenever he could. Spiky could tell that he was hiding something, but he knew better than to bug Jason with any more questions. Spiky decided to wait until after school. He hung back with Jason while Mr. Browser handed over the marbles.

"You must be an expert player," remarked Mr. Browser. "I never had this many marbles in my desk before."

"He *is* an expert," confirmed Spiky. "He wins lots of them every day."

Jason frowned and thanked Mr. Browser as he turned to go.

"You all right now?" asked Mr. Browser.

"Yes, thank you. I'm fine," said Jason.

Spiky walked with him to the school gate. "I'd better come home part of the way with you," he said. "Just in case Barry and his friends try to force you to give back their marbles. You know what they're like."

"Thanks, Spiky," said Jason, and they walked together until they were about halfway to Jason's home. Then Spiky couldn't wait anymore. He hated mysteries and feeling confused and curious about things.

"Look here, Jason, I'm your friend," he began. "Something funny happened when that comet was mentioned. You can't deny it. You looked like you were about to flake out and fall flat on the floor or something! You can tell me, Jason. I promise I won't tell anyone else, not even my own mom and dad. I swear!"

Jason looked Spiky straight in the eye. His own eyes were swimming with tears.

"You *are* my friend, Spiky. I've never had a friend like you," he said. "I'm supposed to keep this a secret, but I don't care. I'm so alone down here, Spiky." Jason's shoulders were shaking. "I don't come from Endfield. I come from the tail of that comet Mr. Browser was talking about this afternoon!"

The Confession 7

It was Spiky's turn to feel very odd this time. He leaned against a garden wall and stared at Jason, who was not the type to joke around.

"Come from where?" he mumbled.

"From a comet. You people call it Halley's Comet," said Jason. "Are you all right, Spiky?"

"Yeah, I'm all right," answered Spiky, pushing himself off the wall. "But you heard what Selwyn Jordan said about comets. There's nothing solid about them. Maybe just some gases. Come off it, Jason!"

Spiky beat himself on the head with his fists. Then he pulled his mouth open wide and grinned at Jason with rolling eyeballs. This horrible expression was Spiky's usual reaction to anything crazy.

Jason didn't seem upset. "You're right. Comets are practically nothing," he agreed.

"Well then," said Spiky, "let's forget it and just go home."

"You see, in the first place we didn't come from a comet," continued Jason. "We just joined it."

"But you just told me you came from a comet!" Spiky shouted.

"All right, Spiky, if you don't want to know, that's fine with me," said Jason seriously.

Spiky grabbed him by the arm. "If there's really a true secret to tell, you'd better tell it," he threatened Jason. "Or I'll tell everyone that you're a comet nut!"

"You promised you wouldn't tell anyone, Spiky! And how can I tell you the truth if you won't listen to me?" Jason looked so scared and tense that Spiky tried to calm him down.

"Go ahead then," Spiky said. "But make sure you tell me the truth, not some crazy lie!"

"I promise, Spiky. But I'm going to have to tell you things you've never dreamed of. It's all true. I swear by all of the fifteen planets of my world."

"Fifteen!" Spiky yelled. "There aren't fifteen planets—"

"There you go again. There aren't fifteen planets around your sun. Or at least, you haven't found them yet. But there were fifteen around my sun. Should I go on?"

"Oh yes, go on." Spiky's head was beginning to swim, and his mouth opened wide as he listened to Jason.

"You see, although most comets don't have any solids, Halley's Comet does now. It's because a number of people from our world have joined onto it. We are traveling round and round in the orbit of the comet, looking for somewhere to settle down.

"Maybe you don't know, Spiky, but there are probably a bunch of planets in other galaxies which are very similar to your world in many ways. My father says that your scientists are just beginning to admit that. Well, my family used to live on one of them. My great-grandfather took pictures of it and wrote a description after he had to leave."

"Why did he have to leave?" asked Spiky.

They were walking very slowly down the street. Now and then, Spiky kicked a rock along in front of him.

"Everyone had to leave. Our scientists—who were much more advanced than yours—discovered that our world was beginning to be sucked in toward our sun. It would happen faster and faster, so they said. And, of course, our world would soon become too hot for life to survive on it. So, plans had to be made for everyone to leave. Luckily, we had invented advanced ways of creating food from gases, and we could also grow a lot of food from miniature plants in a very small space. So there was a chance of survival if our people could get away somewhere safely."

"Sounds like a close call," Spiky said to encourage him to go on.

"Yes, very close. My grandfather has told

me how it all happened. He was a kid at the time. Special areas were set up with huge balloon-like structures. They were blown out of a substance much like your plastic materials. Each balloon was equipped with food and what was needed for life. And each balloon could hold about a hundred people. Families were put into the balloons. Then each balloon was fired from a kind of huge rocket base and set off on its journey through space.

"My great-grandfather was put in charge of our balloon. I never saw him because he died a long time ago, and I was born years after that. I have pictures of him, though."

"So you never really saw your real world?" asked Spiky.

"No. And I never will. By now the climate is probably so hot that everything is burned through and through. I'll always feel like I'm part of it, though."

"But how did you find the comet?" asked Spiky impatiently.

"I'm glad you're beginning to believe

me," said Jason with one of his sharp smiles. "My great-grandfather and my grandfather tried and tried to find another world for us. They hoped to find one with a very simple life system. But as far as they traveled, they couldn't find the right thing.

"Meanwhile, up in space, the families in our balloon grew bigger. Even though we could expand the size of the balloon, we really needed more space. We were always on the move, but we couldn't travel far, if you see what I mean.

"We kept up contact with other balloons, and finally, a whole group of balloons agreed to try to break into some new system of planets to find a suitable world. My great-grandfather died before we arrived in your system, but my grandfather is still alive. Now he is helping to organize our explorations."

Spiky was leaning on a lamp post, looking down at his shoes. As Jason talked, Spiky formed pictures in his mind.

"In our wanderings we happened to cross

the path of Halley's Comet. We discovered that we could use the gases in its tail to increase our supplies of food and energy. Hydrogen, sodium and iron have been found in the head of the comet, and some other elements, too. So we were sailing around your planetary system on the tail of the comet looking for somewhere to live when a report came from a scout balloon that the planet you call earth would be an ideal climate for us."

"Earth!" cried Spiky, "that's us. Oh, no!"

Superhuman Powers

○○○○○○○○○○○○○○○○○○○○○○○○○ **8** ○○

Jason wandered in circles around Spiky trying to explain everything.

"Earth, exactly. That's why I'm here!" he went on. "The scientists in the different balloons worked together and tried to find out all they could about Earth.

"We now know that we could take over large parts of it without much trouble. We could easily settle in the seas, the deserts, and the mountains because there would hardly be anyone there to oppose us. We could land in our balloons and quickly get used to the life in these places.

"The areas where lots of people are living worried our experts the most. They did experiments and listened to what was going on. They noticed that every once in a while terrible weapons were being fired. So we had to find out if the people of your world were very fierce, and if we should have to overcome them before we could settle peacefully."

Jason's air of superiority about the advanced knowledge of his scientists annoyed Spiky.

"What? You're thinking of trying to invade us?" he demanded.

"Well," said Jason apologetically, "something would have to be done. We wouldn't want to be blown to bits on landing, would we? But don't worry about the lives of your people. We have far more advanced methods than you earthlings. No one would be actually killed."

"Thank you," said Spiky.

"So the scientists decided that a family would have to be sent on ahead to try and discover as much as possible about life on Earth. Then we could deal with your people as mercifully as possible.

"Also, the family would learn much about how to live on Earth and see whether life here would really be worthwhile. Because of the work my great-grandfather and my grandfather did, my family was chosen to go on ahead.

"One spy already visited this part before we came so that my father would know enough to be able to land in secret and settle down without being noticed. They thought a family would find out the most about life here. My father would learn about men, my mother would get to know the women's way of living, and I would help them learn whether our children would fit in well with earth children. Of course, my father has some other things to do, but I can't tell you about them."

They had been walking slowly for a little while and soon stopped at the curb before crossing the street. The houses, the gardens, the trees, and the cars all looked different to Spiky now. Jason had talked about the world as though it were some strange planet that could be invaded.

"So you're a spy!" said Spiky.

"No, no. We're seeing if we can fit in well," said Jason.

"But your father is!" Spiky insisted.

"Not really. I think he has to perform some sort of experiment to see if your people can be kept peaceful while our landings are going on. That is, if we decide to come. And we're so much more advanced than you are that you should all be pleased if we do come. That's what my father says. We should be a great help to you."

"What nerve!" shouted Spiky.

"You aren't as clever as you think," Jason said, shrugging his shoulders. "My father says you're building weapons that could destroy your own world! What could be more stupid than that?"

Spiky couldn't think of an answer to that. "How long are you going to stay?" he asked instead.

"We might remain until the rest of our people come, if we decide this world's worth living in. Or we may return to make a report on what we've seen."

They had reached Jason's house. When they stopped outside the gate, Jason turned and looked Spiky right in the face.

"Spiky, I honestly hope we do stay," he said. "It's fun to wander through the skies, but, in a way, you can't move very far. See what I mean? Besides, I like your world. There's plenty to do, and the gravity isn't quite as dense as on our balloon. It's much easier to move here. And I like the food, too!"

"I'm glad you like it," Spiky said. "But I still don't understand how you came here if that comet is still such a long way off."

"It is. We won't be anywhere near the earth until about 1985 or 1986," explained Jason. "Right now we're somewhere between your planets Uranus and Saturn. We're on course, though. And about my family getting here, well, it is possible to shoot off small, disposable balloons that can travel far distances.

"We planned to land near a very populated area. But we also had to arrive in secret. So we timed it for the early hours one day on the mudbanks of a river."

"What happened to the balloon?" Spiky asked.

"Oh, it just dissolved and disappeared in the mud," answered Jason.

"Then, how do you expect to go back?" Spiky realized that he had begun to believe what Jason was telling him.

"That's easy. My father will contact the rest of the balloons, and another small one will be sent to get us. But I hope we won't have to go."

Spiky was silent. Now he felt torn between his promise to his friend and a feeling that he must tell someone right away. This could be an extraterrestrial invasion! Thousands of balloons, Spiky thought to himself, carrying over a hundred people in each, would be about a million invaders at least. And if those invaders really had advanced weapons, as Jason had said, then the earth would be conquered! But had Jason really been telling the truth?

"Here, Spiky. Take ten of my marbles," Jason said as they sat down on his front porch. "You've been a good friend to me, and I trust you. Let's forget all about where I come from and just have a good time."

"Sure, Jason. Thanks a lot," said Spiky, taking the marbles and studying them. Jason was being *very* friendly to him. Spiky was beginning to believe that he had to discover what Jason's father was up to.

"Jason," Spiky began, "will you show me all your marbles? You must have won loads of them in the past few weeks. Now I understand that it wasn't luck at all. It's just that you comet people are so superior."

"Yes," Jason said, his blue eyes gleaming. "There's a case full of marbles hidden in the shed in my backyard. I'm keeping them there right now, so that my father and mother don't find out about them. They told me to only play marbles at home because they knew that I would win easily. That might make someone suspect that there was something unusual about me. But I just couldn't resist it, Spiky! It's the one game on earth that we play too. Come on, I'll show you all of them now. I think my mother and father are both out."

Spiky followed him through the gate and down a path along the side of the house. Opening another gate, Jason took him into his backyard where there was an old, broken-down shed.

He wrenched the door open. Inside the shed were a bunch of old boxes and cans of paint. Jason went to a far corner where there was an old suitcase almost hidden under planks of wood and rusty containers.

"My secret hiding place!" said Jason, throwing the last plank off the top of the case. "Open it, Spiky."

Spiky eased the case open. A couple of spiders scattered, and Jason jumped back. "I can't get used to spiders," he muttered.

But Spiky wasn't paying attention to him. He just stared at the wealth of marbles half filling the huge suitcase.

"Wow!" he exclaimed.

"Not bad for a start." said Jason. Suddenly he felt so excited that he plunged both of his arms into the marbles and stirred them around like a giant bowl of pudding.

"A start!" cried Spiky. He had never seen so many marbles all together in one place!

Jason held his hands still, so that the marbles fell together and became silent. When he turned to face Spiky, his eyes were so bright that they seemed like marbles themselves.

"This shows," Jason said, "that we are superior to you ordinary humans—far superior. I'll win all the marbles I want and sell them for a profit. Then when I grow up I'll have learned how to play other games, and I'll win them all, too. When I work I'll be able to take over offices or factories and do whatever I want. I have superhuman powers, Spiky. These marbles prove it!"

Spiky must have looked a little upset by Jason's statement. Jason quickly tried to reassure him.

"Oh, don't worry, Spiky. You're my friend. I'll make sure that you'll be rich and powerful, too! And while you're at Chivvy

Chase School you'll never run out of marbles!"

"Thanks a lot, Jason," said Spiky, and he smiled. But behind his smile Spiky's thoughts chilled him. If Jason was so superior to humans, then all the people from the comet would be superior, too. That would mean the comet people would gradually take over all the power everywhere.

Spiky had to stop them! He had to save everyone from these comet people! Friend or not, it was up to him to expose Jason and his family.

Spiky thought how lucky it was that he, Spiky Jackson, had become Jason's friend. Selwyn Jordan would have spent ages thinking about the problem and might even have gone along with Jason. Michael Fairlie probably would have run straight to Mr. Browser and told him all about it. Then Jason and his family might have gotten scared and just disappeared. But Spiky thought of himself as a boy of action. He wasn't very smart, as Mr. Browser and Mr. Sage sometimes said, but at least Mr. Browser thought of him as lively. He'd even called him by his nickname, Spiky, once.

"Things are never dull when Spiky's around," Mr. Browser had said when Spiky accidentally slung his football cleats around his head, lost control of them, and watched them fly through a classroom window. Spiky was thinking of these things to give himself confidence and courage. Quickly he took the first step toward what he knew he had to do.

Spiky's Secret 9

○○○○○○○○○○○○○○○○○○○○○○○○○ ○○

As Jason lowered the lid on the marbles
Spiky pushed his finger onto the point of a
rusty nail sticking out of one of the planks.

"Ow! My finger's bleeding," he cried out.
"I cut it on this darn nail!"

Jason took one look at the blood and the
nail, and turned even paler than usual. "You
people bleed easily," he observed.

"Do you think your mother could clean it
up for me? Do you have any Band-Aids?"
asked Spiky. "It really hurts and it might get
infected."

"I don't think she's home," said Jason,
"but I can get a key. You can come in and
wash it while I try to find a Band-Aid."

"Thanks a lot, Jason," said Spiky, holding
his bleeding finger in front of him.

He followed Jason to the back door of the

house. Jason bent down to get the key that was tucked under a broken piece of the patio.

Once inside, Spiky let cold water run over his finger. He really was afraid that the rusty nail might cause an infection. Jason came back after a while with a Band-Aid for him. By now Spiky had a clear idea of how to start his investigation.

"Jason," he began, "you were talking a lot of nonsense to me in that shed. I think the marbles have gone to your head. And as for pretending you come from some comet, you must think I'm some kind of idiot to swallow that!"

"I'm sorry I haven't convinced you," said Jason, disappointed. "It happens to be the truth, as you'll find out sooner or later."

"Are you still trying to kid me?" demanded Spiky, and pushed his face right up to Jason's. He put on one of his most threatening expressions.

Jason backed off in surprise. "I'm not kidding, Spiky, honest I'm not!"

Spiky moved closer. "Then prove it, that's what I say. Show me proof, Jason. Being lucky at marbles doesn't mean a thing to me. Show me something else. If you don't I'll tell your dad you've been playing marbles! I'll tell him about that suitcase in the shed!"

Jason shrank away, afraid that Spiky might hit him. All of a sudden he looked so angry.

"But there isn't anything else!" Jason protested. "I only came here with a few marbles. I didn't bring anything from the comet, I swear!"

"Maybe not," said Spiky, still edging forward. "But you said your dad brought a lot of money. And that he would be doing experiments. He must have brought something to experiment with—that's what you said."

Jason didn't answer, so Spiky decided he had to risk it all with another threat.

"Show me your dad's money and what he's brought with him, or I'll tell Barry where your marbles are, besides telling your dad. I'll watch every move you make, Jason. And as soon as I see something strange, I'll report it to Mr. Browser. Now—show me something!"

Jason hesitated, then he said, "Promise, if I show you, you'll keep it secret?"

"If it's worth seeing," Spiky shot back.

"We'll have to hurry, or my mom will be back. There's a case upstairs in the bedroom, underneath the bed. I went there to look at the money one day. You don't want to take any, do you, Spiky? He'll know right away if any is gone. He has it all in neat stacks."

"No, I don't want his money," said Spiky impatiently. "Show it to me, that's all."

He followed Jason up the stairs. The door to the main bedroom was locked, but the key was in the lock, and Jason turned it cautiously. He was afraid to make noise even though no one was in the house.

There was nothing unusual about the bedroom furniture, Spiky decided. Jason moved swiftly to the bed and pulled out a case from underneath it. The case was made of a kind of strange plastic material, but other than that, it looked normal.

"Just a quick look!" said Jason. "It's unlocked."

Spiky bent forward and Jason lifted the lid. The left side of the case was jammed full of packets of money—ten-dollar bills, Spiky noticed.

"It's true!" he whispered, pretending to concentrate on the bills. Jason looked

pleased. And Spiky's eyes took in the right side of the case, where, just as neatly arranged as the bills, were rows of small, brown plastic cubes.

"And what are those?" asked Spiky, trying to look casual.

"Those? They're for his experiments, I think. He's never really told me. I don't think he knows I've seen them."

"Has he used any yet?" Spiky wanted to know.

"I don't think so," answered Jason, studying the neat rows.

Spiky gripped Jason's arm. "Jason! I heard a voice. Can it be your mom?"

Jason dropped the lid of the case and slipped across to listen at the door. In two seconds Spiky opened the case, took out one of the plastic cubes, and silently closed the case again.

"I can't hear anything," said Jason, coming back. "It must have been somebody outside. But we'd better not hang around. I wouldn't want my parents to know I've been looking through their stuff. My dad wouldn't like it."

"Probably not," agreed Spiky. "Thanks a lot for showing me, though. We'd better go downstairs now. I have to get home, too."

Jason was glad that Spiky wanted to hurry. He carefully locked the bedroom door behind them. Downstairs, Spiky was let out at the back door.

"See you tomorrow, Jason," he called out, and ran to the gate.

"Do you believe me now, Spiky?" Jason called after him.

"Maybe," Spiky called back. "Money and a few plastic boxes don't really prove anything. But I'll keep your secret, Jason."

"Thanks!"

By the time Jason had closed the door Spiky was running fast up the street. He turned two corners and dived down a narrow alley near his house before he stopped. Panting, he took the cube out of his pocket and examined it closely. It was light and smooth, and looked like it was made of some kind of plastic.

74

He looked carefully for some way to open it. But all he could find was a small circle on one side. Maybe if you pressed it? Spiky toyed with the idea, then decided to wait.

Spiky thought that the best thing to do would be to show the cube to Mr. Browser in the morning. He could open it in front of him. Then Jason's secret—if there was one—would be out.

When Spiky went to bed that night he put the cube under his pillow. And all through the night he dreamed about wheeling through space in the tail of a comet.

Sleepy School 10

The next morning while Spiky was walking to school with the mysterious cube in his pocket, Mr. Browser and Mr. Sage were already at school getting ready for the superintendent's visit. The principal made a nervous tour of all the classrooms. He wanted to make sure things were neat and clean.

"All set?" he asked Mr. Browser as he entered the classroom. Mr. Browser was hastily filling a space on the wall with some pictures the class had just drawn.

"I think so," said Mr. Browser. He was secretly wondering whether to treat the superintendent to an exciting lesson on magnets or to risk boring him with a safer one on long division.

"Be sure that Anna Cardwell doesn't play around," Mr. Sage warned him. "She can be very fresh at times." Anna had been talking back to Mr. Sage the day before. "And talking back won't go over very well with Mr. Morten," Mr. Sage added.

"I don't think Anna will be much trouble today," replied Mr. Browser, smiling. "For one thing, she won't be here until after recess. She has to go to the dentist for a couple of fillings this morning. That should keep her quiet for most of the day."

"I should hope so," said Mr. Sage. He decided he might as well go on to the next class.

The morning bell rang, and Mr. Browser went out to the playground to call the class inside. Spiky Jackson, thinking about the cube in his pocket, was one of the first to come in. He wanted to avoid Jason. He had been keeping clear of him this morning because he was afraid that Jason might come up to him and demand the cube back. But Jason has been busy, as usual, playing marbles. Maybe his father hadn't discovered yet that one of his cubes was missing.

Spiky was annoyed that Mr. Browser

was on recess duty. That meant he would be late getting back to the classroom, and Spiky wouldn't have time to show him the cube. When he got to his desk, Spiky quickly pulled up the lid and put the little box inside.

"I've won ten more marbles, Spiky!" reported Jason happily, as he passed by. Spiky nodded, feeling sure now that he had not been discovered.

Mr. Browser was much too busy that morning with roll call and other duties to pay attention to anything else. So the cube remained in Spiky's desk while Spiky worked half-heartedly on his math problems in a book called *Working Away*.

Soon Mr. Browser began to talk seriously to the class about long division.

"Simon Jackson!" he called out sharply. "You aren't paying attention. Later on it will be your own fault if you can't do the problems I give you!"

Spiky was annoyed at having been caught. He thought it looked as if he were paying attention. But his mind, of course, was on the mysterious cube. When should he show it to Mr. Browser? Would he have to wait until recess? He tried to concentrate on Mr. Browser's voice.

Then the bell rang for morning assembly. Spiky had to decide whether to leave the cube in his desk or to take it with him to the assembly.

"Stand up!" ordered Mr. Browser. Spiky decided it would be safer to take the cube with him. But Michael Fairlie saw him reach into his desk for the cube.

"What's that, Spiky?" he whispered.

"Nothing," said Spiky defensively. And, of course, Michael was curious.

The class went into the assembly room where each morning all the children in the school had to sit on the floor and listen to a story. Then there was usually a lecture by Mr. Sage on talking in the halls or leaving litter on the playground. This morning Spiky dozed a little, and Michael Fairlie's hand crept nearer and nearer to the pocket with the cube in it.

Just as the story was about to end, Michael's hand slipped into Spiky's pocket and grabbed the cube.

"No!" cried Spiky in panic. Mr. Sage looked up and stopped reading. He waited for silence again. Grinning, Michael teased Spiky by showing him the edge of the cube underneath his hand. Then Michael put the cube in his own pocket, safely out of Spiky's reach.

Mr. Sage handed over the group to Miss Toms, the assistant principal, and then walked out.

"Boys and girls, stand up!" commanded Miss Toms.

Michael teased Spiky again with the cube.

"Give it back!" demanded Spiky, and grabbed Michael's hand.

"Don't try that," whispered Michael, "or I'll squash it!"

Suddenly Jason saw what was going on, and recognized the cube. "No!" he called out. "Be careful! Don't drop that box!"

"Whatever is going on?" demanded Miss Toms from the other end of the hall.

Michael dropped the box—and stepped on it.

"Everyone stand still!" demanded Miss Toms angrily.

"Run!" screamed Jason.

Spiky took one look at Jason's face and knew he'd better run. Jason was out in the hall in a flash. Spiky dashed after him. Mr. Browser ran after both boys with an amazed look on his face. Everyone else just stood still and watched.

"Get them back here, Mr. Browser," called out Miss Toms, trying to show she was still in command. "The rest of you, stay where you are. We'll have to look into this."

Just then everyone in the school, starting with Spiky's class, began acting very strange. At first the class stood still. Then they gradually sank to the floor, as though all the strength had gone out of them. Curling their arms under their heads, they closed their eyes and began to breathe deeply. Quickly, all the other classes and teachers in the assembly room did the same thing.

"What's happening—" began Miss Toms desperately. But her next words turned into a giant yawn, and she sat back down in her chair. She closed her eyes and fell into a deep sleep.

The strange thing was that nobody came around for a long while and noticed this unusual school assembly. The whole school lay there for a full half hour undisturbed until Mr. Morten, the superintendent, arrived.

He stood still at the front door. Not a sound could be heard. He sniffed. Things weren't going quite as he expected. Perhaps the children were all outside having a fire drill.

Quietly, he made his way to the principal's office. The hallway was deserted and quiet. He knocked politely on the secretary's door. No answer. Opening the door, he stared in amazement at something he had never seen before.

Miss Copewell, the secretary, was sitting with her head on the typewriter and her arms around it, sleeping peacefully. At a desk opposite her the librarian was slumped forward with her head resting on a pile of books. Her hand still gripped the school stamp, which she must have brought to the office to use on the books.

Mr. Morten coughed. No response.

"Holy smokes!" he said, which was a very strong thing for him to say in school. He didn't try to disturb the sleeping women. Instead, he knocked on the door to the principal's office. No answer. Opening the door, he found an even more surprising scene. Mr. Sage had his feet on his desk. He was lying back in his swivel chair, hands behind his head, snoring.

"Mr. Sage!" shouted the superintendent.

Mr. Sage did not move. The superintendent looked around the room. Something very odd has happened, he decided.

He left Mr. Sage, hoping to find someone in the school who was awake. He tiptoed along the corridor and opened the assembly room door. There before him lay the children and teachers of Chivvy Chase School. Stretched out, lying there, they looked as if they had all fallen asleep in the assembly at the same time.

At one corner of the room was a door marked "Janitor" which led into the boiler room. Stepping over bodies, Mr. Morten stumbled to this door and flung it open.

He was hardly surprised now to see the janitor sitting there fast asleep. His head was resting on a daily newspaper.

The kitchen was Mr. Morten's last hope. Staggering through the cafeteria to the kitchen door, he pulled it open. The body of a cook, holding a ladle, fell back gently against his feet. She had been lying asleep against the door, and the other workers were

lying against the ovens, cuddling pots and
plates.

A tap was running freely. Mr. Morten was
now so upset that he welcomed the flowing
water as a sign of life. He moved toward it to
get a drink. But before he could reach the
tap, a tingling sensation of tiredness over-
came him. Breathing became too much of an
effort. He slithered down to the floor and fell
asleep.

The Oxygen Eater 11

○○○○○○○○○○○○○○○○○○○○○○○○○○○ ○○

When he ran from the hall, Spiky Jackson was in front of Jason. But by the time they had reached the school gate, he was panting to try and keep up with him. Jason was running as fast as a bullet. His strides were long, and at times he seemed to be running on air. What he had said about earth's gravity flashed through Spiky's mind.

Mr. Browser, struggling behind them and calling out to them, was having great trouble with gravity. Soon both boys turned a corner, and he lost sight of them.

Jason ran up a narrow path between two houses, and Spiky followed him. Suddenly Jason stopped.

"Are we safe now, Jason?" asked Spiky, gulping in air.

"Should be," said Jason.

"What will happen to the others?" Spiky asked.

"They'll look like they've fallen asleep," Jason told him. "They won't be hurt, but they'll be unconscious for at least a couple of hours. Everybody who stays in that building will be. You shouldn't have taken that cube, Spiky!"

"What was in it?" asked Spiky.

"My dad told me the cubes have a gas called Oxygen Eater in them. The gas eats up oxygen fast, so that people quickly lose consciousness. There's just enough left for them to stay alive. My dad will be furious! I never should have shown you those cubes, Spiky. Now I might have ruined his whole experiment!"

"You didn't tell me what was in the cubes," complained Spiky. "I wouldn't have taken one if I'd known."

"Too late now," said Jason bitterly. He stared thoughtfully at his friend. "You'd better come home with me, Spiky, and explain to my mom what's happened."

"Shouldn't we—" began Spiky.

But Jason suddenly grabbed his arm in an iron grip and pulled him along. "I can't take all the blame for this!" he declared. "You're just as much to blame."

Spiky struggled to get away at first. But soon he realized that skinny Jason could call up extra powers of strength as well as speed. He allowed himself to be pulled along the whole way to Jason's house.

Jason's mother was in the living room watching television and reading a book at the same time.

"Jason, why are you home so early?" she asked when they came in.

"It's the Oxygen Eater, Mom. Spiky Jackson set a cube off in school. They're all lying there unconscious now!"

"Oh, Jason, no!" Jason's mother stood up. "You could have ruined us!" she gasped. "Take Spiky upstairs while I call your father. Does anyone else know what has happened?"

"Not really," said Jason. "Especially if the cube has disintegrated."

"It should have. But, Jason, you've upset the whole plan. I don't know what your father will say when I tell him. I expect we'll have to leave at once!"

"I trusted Spiky," said Jason. "How could I know he would steal one of the cubes! I didn't tell him what was in it."

"Oh, Jason, and I liked this world so much!" his mother said.

"So did I," said Jason sadly.

"Now, take Spiky upstairs this minute," she commanded.

"But I don't want to go," protested Spiky.

"Do as I say!" yelled Jason's mother. "In fact, I'm coming with you. Up you go!"

"In there!" Jason's mother ordered him. She pushed Spiky into a small bedroom and locked the door. "Jason, you keep guard! I pray that I can get through to you father immediately. Oh, Jason, Jason. . . ."

From behind the locked door Spiky tried to listen to what was being said. Suddenly Jason's mother seemed to be talking gibberish. But Jason understood her. He answered in the same weird way. Spiky realized that it must be the language of their own world.

"Let me out!" shouted Spiky, horrified.

"Stay there until my father comes!" Jason shouted back. "We'll see what he wants to do."

Spiky pressed his ear against the keyhole, and a few moments later heard the sound of Jason's mother dialing a telephone number. To his despair, when she started to speak it was again in the strange foreign language she had used when talking to Jason.

The receiver clicked down, and Jason's mother came upstairs. Again Spiky listened. The strange new language they were using frightened him as much as being locked in the room did. He began to realize that he was now in the power of beings from another world.

"You can't keep me prisoner here!" he shouted, and began kicking the bottom of the door with all of his might.

"It's no good doing that," Jason's mother said in English. "You'll have to come back with us. That's what Jason's father said. You know too much now. I'm very sorry, and it's mostly Jason's fault. But now it can't be helped. We can't have people down here suspecting that we're going to occupy this planet."

"Back with you! Where to?" demanded Spiky frantically, though in his heart he already knew the answer.

"I thought Jason had told you that. It won't be so bad. Besides," she went on in a motherly tone of voice, "after a few years we may very well come back to earth! That is, of course, if all goes well and nobody down here suspects we are coming. If things don't go well, we may have to wait until the next time round."

"But that could be seventy-five years later!" Spiky wailed, becoming frantic. "No way! I don't want to leave the earth. Jason, you like it here, don't you? Why don't you stay here with me? Who wants to go roaming around space in a weird balloon in the tail of a comet? Come on, Jason. Make your dad let you stay with me!"

"Come downstairs with me, Jason," said his mother in English. "We'll have something to eat, and I'll have to get ready for the journey. We'll have to walk out over that dreadful mud again, I suppose."

Spiky heard their footsteps as they went down the stairs and into the kitchen. A door closed and there was silence.

Spiky cried quietly and felt very sorry for himself. No one in the world had ever been in a worse situation than the one he was in now. Plenty of people had been kidnapped, but no one had ever faced the danger of having to go trailing around space in the tail of a comet.

Spiky beat his hands on the door and sobbed his heart out. Then he tried to pull himself together and think of what he could do in the few hours he had left on earth.

Escape from the bedroom was impossible. And they would probably guard him carefully on his way to the strange balloon that would come to take them away.

He took out his pocket diary, which he always carried with him. In capital letters he wrote on a blank page:

```
HELP! SIMON JACKSON BEING
KIDNAPPED. LOOK FOR A
BALLOON-LIKE OBJECT
SOMEWHERE NEAR THE PIER.
DON'T LET THEM TAKE ME
TO ANOTHER WORLD! BEWARE
OF HALLEY'S COMET!
```

He crumpled up the page and put it in his pocket. Maybe he could drop it in a good place later on. Perhaps somebody would find it. Even if he couldn't be saved, the message might make somebody suspicious. Spiky felt faint, but he also felt noble. He was doing all he could to save our civilization from a comet invasion.

He lay down on Jason's bed and stared at the ceiling. He tried to think of some hopeful thought. Mr. Browser had been following them, he remembered. But he probably went back to school to figure out what the Oxygen Eater had done to all the children and teachers.

Then Spiky heard the sound of running feet on the stairs. Jason's dad was home. He was talking excitedly to his wife in that strange language.

A minute later Jason barged into the room, pulled a suitcase out from under the bed, and threw clothes in it from a drawer. Spiky sprang from the bed and made a dash for the door.

"Sorry, kid!" said Jason's father. He was a stocky, dark haired man with eyes as intense as Jason's "You have spoiled our whole expedition. And you know too much. You'll have to come with us. If people here don't find out about us, maybe you'll be able to return to earth in a few years. But now you must come with us!"

"Isn't there any other way?" pleaded Spiky.

"The only other way, my boy, would be to get rid of you for good, if you understand what I mean. We don't want to do that, because none of this would have happened if Jason hadn't given the game away. I warned our people of the danger of bringing a child with us! Still, Jason needs a friend, and he says he likes you. He's a little lonely up there in space, I guess."

"But," Jason's father went on, "we are due to leave earth in half an hour. We can't waste any more time talking. Follow me to the car right now. Jason, hold on to him and don't let go!"

"Jason," Spiky whispered as they went down the stairs, "be a pal and let me get away!"

Jason didn't even answer. His blue eyes were staring straight ahead. It seemed like he was already halfway out of this world. Spiky was dragged to the car with Jason on one side of him and Jason's father on the other.

"Help!" he shouted. "I'm being—"

A firm hand closed over his mouth. The street was silent. Soon the last chance to escape was gone.

Spiky was pushed into the back seat of the car between Jason and his mother. The suitcases were loaded into the trunk, and Spiky set off on his last ride through the town.

"You look pale," said Jason's mother. Maybe she was feeling a little sorry for him. "Open the window, Jason."

Jason opened the window, but fresh air was not going to make Spiky feel any better.

Good-bye home! Good-bye school! Good-bye world! he thought. He had once wished that he could be an astronaut. But now he was about to become an astronaut without hope of ever coming back to earth. Spiky was sure he wouldn't survive the flight up to Halley's Comet. He could never live for years in some air-conditioned balloon! Spiky wished he had never met Jason.

"Can't I even send a message to my mom and dad?" he asked in a sad tone of voice.

Jason's father shook his head firmly.

Dazed, Spiky lay back and watched his world go by. The car turned a corner. There was Anna Cardwell coming down the sidewalk toward them. For a moment Spiky thought he was dreaming, or that he had already gone out of his mind. Anna Cardwell should be lying in the assembly room at school, still sleeping from the Oxygen Eater!

Then he remembered. Anna had been absent that morning because she had to go to the dentist! She must be on her way back to school.

"Anna, help!" he yelled as the car came alongside her. Spiky took the ball of crumpled-up paper and flung it through the window. He saw the paper drop into the gutter just beside Anna's feet. For a second, he could see the surprised look on her face.

Had she recognized him? Had she heard him? And most important of all, would she pick up the piece of paper and read it? Before Spiky could tell, Jason's angry father speeded up the car, and Jason's mother closed the window.

Not one more word of English was spoken as Spiky was hurried toward his awful fate out on the mud flats by the river.

The Chase

12

Anna was in a happy mood trying not to step on the cracks in the sidewalk as she made her way back to school. Now that her toothache was gone—or just numb—she wanted to take her time. She wouldn't mind missing Mr. Browser's math lesson.

When she heard Spiky's cry and saw his frightened face, she stopped and stared after the car. She saw him throw a small ball of paper out the window. Now it was rolling in the gutter.

What was Spiky doing in a car at this time of day? There had been another kid, someone smaller, sitting next to him in the back seat—it was Jason Taylor, of course!

Now Anna was really curious. She had been watching Jason's marble games with great interest. He was unusual! But why weren't Jason and Spiky in school? Why was Spiky looking so scared?

Then she picked the paper up and un-rolled it.

HELP! SIMON JACKSON BEING KIDNAPPED. LOOK FOR A BALLOON-LIKE OBJECT. SOMEWHERE NEAR THE PIER. DON'T LET THEM TAKE ME TO ANOTHER WORLD! BEWARE OF HALLEY'S COMET!

Anna read the message twice and decided to run all the way back to school. When she arrived she was surprised to see two police cars standing there.

"Where have you been?" demanded the policeman guarding the main entrance.

"To the dentist," answered Anna.

"Oh, so you don't know anything about what's going on here?"

"No. How could I know?" Anna felt confused.

"All right, all right, go on in," the policeman said.

At the foot of the stairs Mr. Browser was talking with Mr. Sage. Both of them looked very serious.

"So you lost them both?" Mr. Sage was saying. "Do you have any idea which direction they were going in? Jason's house? Or maybe Simon Jackson's?"

"Could have been either," replied Mr. Browser. "They both live in that direction."

"Well, now that everyone seems to have recovered, I suppose it's our responsibility to find out what those stupid boys are up to," said Mr. Sage. "I don't want the police involved yet, because I can't believe those boys were responsible for this. The whole school losing consciousness! I still think that it might have been something to do with fumes from the boiler."

"Maybe," said Mr. Browser doubtfully. Then he looked at Anna. "Hello. Back from the dentist? You really were better off there, you know. Everybody's been falling asleep here. I had to wake them up when I came back from searching for Simon and Jason."

"Yes, yes," said Mr. Sage irritably. He didn't like Mr. Browser to talk about such unusual matters with a child.

"But Mr. Sage," Anna burst out, "I just saw Spiky—I mean Simon—and Jason in a car. And Spiky threw this message out to me. It doesn't make sense, Mr. Browser, but he looked awfully upset!"

She handed the note to Mr. Browser, and together he and Mr. Sage read it.

"Nonsense," exclaimed Mr. Sage.

"You say Simon looked upset?" asked Mr. Browser.

"Yes, very upset, Mr. Browser. He looked scared stiff!"

"Could you recognize the car they were in?" Mr. Browser asked Anna.

"Yes, I think it was Jason's father's car."

"Do you think," Mr. Browser asked Mr. Sage, "that it would be worthwhile if I took

Anna and a couple of other kids in my car along the river to see if we can spot them?"

"Yes, I suppose you might as well," Mr. Sage said, shaking his head. "But can't you go on your own?"

"The more sharp eyes I have to help me, the better," said Mr. Browser.

"All right, then," Mr. Sage agreed. "I'll take your class until you come back. Which children do you want to take with you?"

"Fairlie and Jordan. And Anna to recognize the car."

"I'll send them out to the parking lot," said Mr. Sage. "But I think you'll be wasting your time. Jackson may well be up to one of his tricks."

Two minutes later Mr. Browser was driving out of the school parking lot with Anna, Michael Fairlie, and Selwyn Jordan in his car. Michael and Selwyn listened carefully as Anna explained what she had seen. Then Selwyn told Anna what had happened that morning in the assembly room.

Mr. Browser turned a corner and they

were on the long road which ran along the river docks.

"Now, all of you keep your eyes open," he demanded. "Shout as soon as you see anything suspicious, and I'll slow down. We must look for the car."

In five minutes they reached the dock. After they'd gone about a mile along the road Anna shouted, "That's it! Right by the lamp post."

Mr. Browser slowed down and parked behind the yellow car Anna had pointed out.

"It's empty," said Selwyn.

"There they go!" cried Anna. "Four of them, right out there on the mud!"

"Whatever are they doing?" muttered Mr. Browser as they tumbled out of the car and headed toward the mud.

"One of them's being dragged," declared Anna, squinting.

"Yes!" said Selwyn. "That must be Spiky. There's a man and a woman, and the smaller boy must be Jason."

"I don't like the way that boy's being

dragged along," said Mr. Browser. "It almost looks as though they're trying to drown him. I can't believe it! But we'd better find out. Take your shoes and socks off. We're going after them!"

They had to move slowly, their feet sinking deep into the mud.

"Keep going!" shouted Mr. Browser, whose longer strides had helped him to stay in the lead. "It looks as though Spiky has fallen over. Look! They're picking him up from the mud!"

"They're taking him somewhere he doesn't want to go," said Selwyn solemnly.

" 'Course they are!" puffed Anna. "Anyone can see that!"

"Hurry!" Mr. Browser urged them, "or we may be too late to find out."

"We're gaining on them," Michael declared.

"Yes, because they've stopped," said Mr. Browser. "They're waiting for something—but what?"

"Spiky! We're coming!" shouted Anna as loud as she could.

Spiky heard her and turned around.

"They're taking me—" he began. But Jason's father put his hand over Spiky's mouth.

"Where could they be taking him?" Mr. Browser wondered aloud.

"To a comet, or something," said Anna. "Remember how Jason almost passed out when we talked about Halley's Comet?"

"You're nuts," commented Michael.

"Maybe she isn't nuts," said Selwyn Jordan quietly. "There's something in the air up above us. It looks like a balloon."

They all looked up. Out of nothing a huge round shape was forming above Jason and Spiky. Anna, Michael, and Selwyn stopped to watch in amazement, but Mr. Browser splashed forward frantically.

"Don't go, Spiky!" Mr. Browser shouted. "We're coming!"

A door seemed to open in the side of the strange shape. The whole, hazy thing was coming down to the mud.

Jason and his family moved forward. But Spiky, in one last-ditch effort, flung himself sideways. He knocked into Jason's father and threw him off balance.

"Help me! I don't want to go!" screamed Spiky, and fell flat in the mud.

Jason's father urged Jason and his mother into the strange craft. He made one more effort to pull Spiky with him. Then he ran because Mr. Browser was at his heels.

"Spiky!" called Jason from the balloon, "look after your world for us. We may be back one day!"

He disappeared inside. Jason's father paused in the doorway and took something from his pocket. He crushed it in his hand and flung it toward Mr. Browser. Then the door closed and the balloon took off. Before it was a hundred feet in the air it began to disappear. In a few seconds it vanished.

"It's all right, Spiky!" shouted Mr. Browser. He bent down to try and pull Spiky out of the mud.

But suddenly Spiky became hazy to Mr. Browser's eyes. The teacher stumbled and fell flat in the mud. He lay alongside Spiky in a deep sleep.

Anna, Selwyn, and Michael were running to Spiky's rescue. But suddenly they gave up, swaying gently sideways and collapsing in the mud.

The breeze carried the Oxygen Eater this way and that. It thinned out, but its work had been done. The only witnesses to the amazing balloon holding Jason and his family were lying unconscious in the mud.

The river was rising now. In a half hour the five bodies would be completely covered by water. There would be no one left alive to warn the world of the danger—invasion from Halley's Comet in 1986.

The water was already lapping around Mr. Browser's head.

The Only
Evidence

○○○○○○○○○○○○○○○○○○○○○○○○○ **13** ○○

Mr. Sage looked after Mr. Browser's class
until afternoon recess. Then he returned to
his office. A puzzled policeman and a doctor
were still there.

"Any news?" asked the principal.

"Nothing," said the detective in charge.
"We've searched the building completely,
and examined the assembly room for any
signs of a chemical substance. But there's
nothing at all. And the box Michael Fairlie
talked about doesn't seem to exist."

"You can never be sure whether or not
children are imagining things," observed
Mr. Sage in a knowing manner.

"True," agreed the detective. "We'd like
another word with Mr. Browser."

"Well—er—Mr. Browser has gone in his
car to try and find the boys," explained Mr.

Sage. "A girl called Anna Cardwell was coming back to school from the dentist's, and she saw Jason and Simon Jackson in Jason's father's car. It seems that Simon threw a note out to her. A lot of nonsense, I thought when I saw it, but Browser decided he'd go with some children to try and find them."

"Where is this note?" asked the detective briskly.

"Browser has it," replied the principal.

"We should have been told all of this right away," the detective said. "This could be a kidnapping. We tried to check up on this Jason kid and his family. We found nothing. Did this note give any indication of where the boys were being taken?"

"Yes, along the river somewhere," recalled Mr. Sage. "There was some nonsense about a balloon, and the Jackson boy was frightened of being taken to some place called Comet. But that sounds like childish nonsense to me."

"I'm going with two men to check on things by the river," said the detective.

The police car roared off and filled the air with the noise of its siren. In less than ten minutes it was patrolling the river front. The detective had been given a description of Mr. Browser's old car.

"The river's rising," said the detective. "I can't see any boats out there."

"Over there!" called out the policeman in the back seat. He pointed to the other side of the dock.

"What's over there?" demanded the detective."

"I thought I saw something rising up into the sky," explained the policeman. "But there's nothing there now. It's vanished completely."

The detective looked back at the policeman through his mirror.

"Don't try too hard," he said sarcastically. "This morning's ordeal was mysterious enough, without adding to it."

"Wait!" shouted one policeman. "I think I can see that teacher's car parked by the road ahead of us."

"That's it!" confirmed the other.

The detective studied the river through binoculars. Then he gradually took in the mud and the riverbank which was being flooded by the rising water.

"There's someone out there!" he shouted. "A man, flat out in the water. And a child. Yes, it's them. Five bodies, all lying in the mud! The water's just reached them. Let's go! It may be a matter of life or death!"

Their feet were sucked down by the mud like runners in a nightmare. Once or twice one of the men lost a shoe. But they didn't stop their headlong dash.

The detective found Anna lying face down in the water and pulled her out. Spiky, Michael, and Selwyn were each carried back. Then they rescued Mr. Browser who was lying face up, barely floating. Soon signs of life were reported in each victim.

"Thank heavens, they're breathing now," sighed the detective.

Although the five bodies were alive, the policemen were puzzled because they remained unconscious. They tried everything they could think of to wake them. But the Oxygen Eater was still at work.

"It's as though they're drugged," said the detective shrewdly.

Half an hour later, Anna Cardwell, who had been farthest away from Jason's father when he had crushed the cube, came to her senses.

"Is Spiky still here?" she asked, sitting up. "Who's Spiky?"

"That's him, Spiky Jackson," she said, pointing. "Thank goodness they didn't take him!"

"Take him where?" the detective asked.

"Into that thing that came for Jason," said Anna. "They wanted to take Spiky with them."

"Oh yes," agreed the detective. "And where to, may I ask?"

"I don't really know," she admitted, shaking her head. "He wrote something about a comet, but—"

"Ah, yes. Was that the name of the boat that came to take them away?" asked the detective.

"It wasn't a boat," said Anna. "It was some kind of balloon. Can I go back now? I'm soaked."

Spiky, Michael, Selwyn, and Mr. Browser were all sitting up now. They looked dazed and confused. The detective thought about Anna's answers to his questions. He decided it would be better to wait awhile for more information.

They all drove back to the school so parents could be called and maybe more questions could be answered.

"They come from Halley's Comet," Spiky insisted. "They're only living there until they can find somewhere better. Jason liked our world, so they may invade us at any time."

Spiky felt breathless, but he went on. "They'll come when Halley's Comet is nearest to us. They'll land in their space balloons and take us by surprise. But if they think we're ready for them, they're going to wait until the next time the comet comes around."

The detective kept making comments like, "You like science fiction, don't you, Spiky?" and, "Been reading a lot of comics lately?"

Then Spiky wouldn't tell them any more. They turned to Mr. Browser and asked him if Spiky read a lot of comics and science fiction books. But Mr. Browser said no. As far as he knew, Spiky didn't read very much at all.

The police kept an eye on Chivvy Chase School for a while. They kept trying to find evidence to prove that Jason had been gifted with special powers, as Spiky insisted. When they couldn't find anything, they were very pleased.

But during one interview with the detective Spiky's face lit up.

"Thought of something, son?" asked the detective.

"Yes," said Spiky. "If we could go to the house where Jason lived, I could give you proof that Jason was unusual."

"All right, Jason's father was only renting the house, so we can ask the owner to open it up for us."

"Oh, we don't need to go inside," said Spiky. "All we need to do is to look in the shed at the bottom of the garden."

"We'll go now," said the detective.

"Better let Browser go with you," said Mr. Sage. "He's been mixed up in this."

Mr. Sage was eager to forget about Jason and the trouble he'd caused. The superintendent had told him he would come back to the school again on what he called "a more normal day."

Mr. Browser left his classroom to go with Spiky and the detective to Jason's old house.

"Now, Simon, take us right to the evidence," commanded the detective.

Spiky led them to the old case in the corner and struggled to pull up the lid. Eagerly the detective helped him. The lid sprung open, and there was the evidence!

"Marbles!" yelled the detective. "Hundreds of marbles!" He looked angrily at Spiky. "Why have you brought me all this way to look at a suitcase full of marbles?" he demanded.

"Jason won them all," said Spiky. "All he cared about was marbles. No one could beat him at it. He had special powers. That's the evidence you wanted."

The detective let the lid of the case drop, and threw up his hands in disbelief.

"A load of marbles! That's supposed to be my evidence!" he complained. "What can

a load of marbles possibly have to do with it?"

He turned to Mr. Browser, hoping he would explain all this craziness.

"Jason was extremely good at winning marbles," admitted Mr. Browser. "He used to ask me to look after them for him."

"Oh, yeah? But you aren't trying to tell me that just because Jason was good at marbles he came from outer space, are you?"

Mr. Browser didn't like to argue with people, especially detectives and policemen. Besides, the truth about Jason and his mysterious powers was far from clear to him.

"I'm not trying to convince you," he admitted. "But I don't think that adults should ignore the importance of marbles as a game. Marbles go out of style sometimes, but then suddenly they're back. And I must say I've never seen so many marbles in one place before."

"Well, I admit I used to have some good ones when I was a kid," began the detective. "But I really can't waste my time here any longer. Tell you what, since the marbles belonged to a boy in your class, it would be a shame to waste them. Why don't you take them to school and give them out to the kids who lost them?"

"Good idea," said Spiky.

"I'll arrange to have them picked up," said Mr. Browser.

The detective smiled as he drove them back to school and went on his way.

o o o

Mr. Browser became very popular when he passed out the marbles to all the students in his class. Gradually the strange adventure with Jason was forgotten or explained away.

But one person will never forget. Spiky Jackson is waiting for the arrival of Halley's Comet in 1986. Even if the earth is not invaded, he will still be wondering about it as it shoots through space. Maybe his friend Jason is up there playing his amazing game of "planets."

When will the comet people try to find a new home in the world Jason liked so much? Spiky looks up at the stars each clear night . . . and waits and wonders.

PHILIP CURTIS

is a deputy headmaster of a junior school in England. He has written many articles for educational journals and is the author of short stories, plays, and books for children including *Invasion of the Brain Sharpeners* and *Invasion from Below the Earth,* two more science fiction Capers from Knopf.

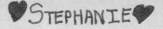

♥STEPHANIE♥

More Science Fiction and Fantasy Capers from Knopf!

Capers are . . .

"That rare series of fast-reading, high motivational
books which should be among the 'basics' in our schools.
Students will grab these books off the shelves
in any classroom or library."

—M. JERRY WEISS,
Distinguished Service Professor
of Communications,
Jersey City State College